MIX
Papier aus verantwortungsvollen Quellen
Paper from responsible sources
FSC® C105338

Ava Tress

The Effect of Empowering Leadership on Work Engagement in an Organizational Change Environment

An Investigation of the Mediating Roles of Self-Efficacy and Self-Esteem

Anchor Academic Publishing

Tress, Ava: The Effect of Empowering Leadership on Work Engagement in an Organizational Change Environment. An Investigation of the Mediating Roles of Self-Efficacy and Self-Esteem, Hamburg, Anchor Academic Publishing 2017

Buch-ISBN: 978-3-96067-149-7
PDF-eBook-ISBN: 978-3-96067-649-2
Druck/Herstellung: Anchor Academic Publishing, Hamburg, 2017

Bibliografische Information der Deutschen Nationalbibliothek:
Die Deutsche Nationalbibliothek verzeichnet diese Publikation in der Deutschen Nationalbibliografie; detaillierte bibliografische Daten sind im Internet über http://dnb.d-nb.de abrufbar.

Bibliographical Information of the German National Library:
The German National Library lists this publication in the German National Bibliography. Detailed bibliographic data can be found at: http://dnb.d-nb.de

All rights reserved. This publication may not be reproduced, stored in a retrieval system or transmitted, in any form or by any means, electronic, mechanical, photocopying, recording or otherwise, without the prior permission of the publishers.

Das Werk einschließlich aller seiner Teile ist urheberrechtlich geschützt. Jede Verwertung außerhalb der Grenzen des Urheberrechtsgesetzes ist ohne Zustimmung des Verlages unzulässig und strafbar. Dies gilt insbesondere für Vervielfältigungen, Übersetzungen, Mikroverfilmungen und die Einspeicherung und Bearbeitung in elektronischen Systemen.

Die Wiedergabe von Gebrauchsnamen, Handelsnamen, Warenbezeichnungen usw. in diesem Werk berechtigt auch ohne besondere Kennzeichnung nicht zu der Annahme, dass solche Namen im Sinne der Warenzeichen- und Markenschutz-Gesetzgebung als frei zu betrachten wären und daher von jedermann benutzt werden dürften.

Die Informationen in diesem Werk wurden mit Sorgfalt erarbeitet. Dennoch können Fehler nicht vollständig ausgeschlossen werden und die Diplomica Verlag GmbH, die Autoren oder Übersetzer übernehmen keine juristische Verantwortung oder irgendeine Haftung für evtl. verbliebene fehlerhafte Angaben und deren Folgen.

Alle Rechte vorbehalten

© Anchor Academic Publishing, Imprint der Diplomica Verlag GmbH
Hermannstal 119k, 22119 Hamburg
http://www.diplomica-verlag.de, Hamburg 2017
Printed in Germany

List of Contents

List of Contents	II
List of Abbreviations	III
List of Figures	IV
List of Tables	V
Abstract	1
1 Introduction	1
2 Literature Review and Hypothesis Development	2
2.1 Empowering Leadership and Work Engagement	4
2.2 The Mediating Roles of Self-Efficacy	5
2.2.1 Empowering Leadership and Self-Efficacy	5
2.2.2 Self-Efficacy and Work Engagement	6
2.3 The Mediating Roles of Self-Esteem	7
2.3.1 Empowering Leadership and Self-Esteem	8
2.3.2 Self-Esteem and Work Engagement	8
3 Method	9
3.1 Sample and Data Collection	9
3.2 Measures	10
4 Results	11
4.1 Sample Characteristics	11
4.2 Hypothesis Testing	12
4.2.1 Direct Effect of Empowering Leadership on Work Engagement	13
4.2.2 Mediating Effects of Self-Efficacy and Self-Esteem	13
5 Discussion	14
6 Limitations and Future Research Directions	15
7 Conclusion	16
Appendix	VI
List of Literature	XII

List of Abbreviations

cf.	confer
CSE	Certificate of Secondary Education
e.g.	exemple gratia
EL	Empowering Leadership
GCSE	General Certificate of Secondary Education
i.e.	id est
SLF	Self-Efficacy
SLS	Self-Esteem
WE	Work Engagement

List of Figures

Figure 1: The JD-R Model (van den Heuvel et al., 2009, p. 126) VI

Figure 2: The expanded JD-R Model (in part) by Xanthopoulou et al. (2007, p. 135) .. VI

Figure 3: The Personal Resources Adaption Model by van den Heuvel et al. (2009,

   p. 138) VII

Figure 4: Scatterplot of the EL - WE Relationship (SPSS-Output) VIII

Figure 5: Final Model (Partial Mediation) 14

List of Tables

Table 1: Internal Consistency: Cronbach´s alpha……………………..............................VII

Table 2: Descriptive Statistics – Frequencies (Gender, Age, Education)……...........…..11

Table 3: Descriptive Statistics (Gender, Age, Education)………………...........………..12

Table 4: Means, Standard Deviations, Internal Consistencies (Cronbach's α on the diagonal) and Correlations among the variables……..........…………………..12

Table 5: Linear Regression – Direct Effect of EL on WE (Overall Model)…….............IX

Table 6: Linear Regression – Direct Effect of EL on WE (ANOVA)..............................IX

Table 7: Linear Regression – Direct Effect of EL on WE (Coefficients)........................IX

Table 8: Linear Regression – Effect of SLF on EL and WE (Overall Model...................X

Table 9: Linear Regression – Effect of SLF on EL and WE (ANOVA)............................X

Table 10: Linear Regression – Effect of SLF on EL and WE (Coefficients)....................X

Table 11: Linear Regression – Effect of SLS on EL and WE (Overall Model)...............XI

Table 12: Linear Regression – Effect of SLS on EL and WE (ANOVA)..........................XI

Table 13: Linear Regression – Effect of SLS on EL and WE (Coefficients)...................XI

Abstract

The Change Management Study investigated the relationship between Empowering Leadership and Work Engagement. Consistent with social learning and social identity theories, Self-Efficacy was examined as a mediator of the Empowering Leadership to Work Engagement relationship. Results from 147 participants showed that Empowering Leadership is positively and significantly related to Work Engagement and that this relationship is mediated by Self-Efficacy. Furthermore, the influence of Self-Esteem on the Empowering Leadership to Work Engagement relationship was investigated. As the internal consistency coefficient of Self-Esteem was unacceptable, this effect had to be neglected in the current study. Results, Limitations and Future Research Directions are discussed.

1 Introduction

As modern organizations seek for changes to enhance their competitive positions and their survivability in global markets (Higgs & Rowland, 2005), the successful implementation of organizational change has become an important management task. But still, many companies are unable to succeed in change processes (Higgs & Rowland, 2005; Jaros, 2010). Failures show, that there is considerable room for researchers to provide insights into opportunities for improving the success of organizational change events (Parish, Cadwallader & Busch, 2007). Given the fact, that individuals are the most important units in organizational change (Graetz & Smith, 2010), a successful implementation requires employees' acceptance and support (Fedor, Caldwell & Herold, 2006). Hence, employees' positive attitudes and their Work Engagement are considered to be fundamental requirements (Fedor et al., 2006). Nevertheless, there is limited understanding of the multitudinous factors associated with employees' decision to support organizational change (Lamm & Gordon, 2010).

Basically, organizational change is stressful as it requires the readiness to embrace change and the readjustment of employees' routine tasks. In this regard, leadership is considered to be one of the most important variables affecting the attitudinal dimension of organizational processes (Jaskyte, 2003). Yousef (2000), also, identified leadership as a critical element in organizational change. In respect of the types of leadership behavior and their exchange relationship with followers, several reviews and meta-analyses have shown, that Empowering Leadership can result in individual, group and unit performance beyond expectations.

Empowering Leadership implies sharing power to foster employees' motivation and engagement in their work (Kirkman & Rosen, 1999). It is the process of establishing conditions that enable sharing power with an employee by indicating the significance of the employee's job, providing greater decision-making autonomy, demonstrating trust in the employee's capabilities and providing each employee with the opportunity to act as flexibly as circumstances allow for (Arnold et al., 2000). Thus, Empowering Leadership emerges when supervisors foster trust-based relationships with followers, show interest in their personal problems, facilitate participative decision-making and coach them to be more self-reliant (Kirkman & Rosen, 1999). These specifications show, that this leadership style is highly relevant to Employee Work Engagement.

However, relatively few studies have tested how and why Empowering Leadership relates to Follower Work Engagement in organizational change environments.

In this context, students from the University of Potsdam came up with the Change Management Study, which is explicated in the following.

The purpose of this term paper is to examine how Empowering Leadership affects Employee Work Engagement in organizational change processes by investigating the roles of two potential mediators, Self-Efficacy and Self-Esteem.

2 Literature Review and Hypothesis Development

The following course of action is based on the assumptions of the Job Demands-Resources Model (JD-R Model) and its extended forms (Bakker & Demerouti, 2007). The JD-R Model provides a framework for understanding the processes by which work environment factors determine well-being and motivation (i.e. Work Engagement) through job demands and job resources (see *Figure 1* in the **Appendix**).

Hakanen, Bakker, & Schaufeli (2006) stated, that job resources (e.g. leadership behavior) are considered to be the most important predictors, when it comes to explaining differences in Employee Work Engagement.

Xanthopoulou et al. (2007) expanded the JD-R Model by examining how personal resources affect relations of the model's processes (see *Figure 2* in the **Appendix**). Personal resources are defined as factors of the self, that refer to resiliency and to individuals' sense of their ability to control and impact upon their organizational environment successfully (Hobfoll, Johnson, Ennis & Jackson, 2003). They included three typical personal resources, namely, Self-Efficacy (Bandura, 1977), organizational-based Self-Esteem (Pierce et al., 1989) and Optimism.

Previous studies have shown that these personal resources are not only related to stress resilience, but also have positive effects on employees' well-being at the workplace (Pierce et al., 1989). Additionally, they concluded that these resource levels are cultivated by environmental factors (i.e. leadership behavior during organizational change).

Based on these findings, Pierce and Gardner (2004) suggested, that personal resources mediate the relationship between resourceful work characteristics (i.e. leadership style: e.g. perceived fairness, support, influence) and employee motivation / attitudes (i.e. Work Engagement). That supports the idea of mediating effects by personal resources in the relationship between Empowering Leadership and Work Engagement.

In the context of organizational change, van den Heuvel et al. (2009) came up with an extended concept of the JD-R Model, namely, the Personal Resources Adaption Model (see *Figure 3* in the **Appendix**). When it comes to understanding organizational change events, employees' personal resources are considered to be the most relevant factors, rather than job resources. This model suggests a reciprocal relationship between employees' personal resources (Self-Efficacy and Self-Esteem in this case) and the work environment (leadership behavior during organizational change).

Based on the findings above, this term paper derives three hypotheses, which are explicated in the following.

2.1 Empowering Leadership and Work Engagement

Empowering Leadership aims at the development of follower self-management / self-leadership skills. The historical roots of Empowering Leadership are found in behavioral self-management (Mahoney & Thoresen, 1974), social cognitive theory (Bandura, 1986), cognitive behavior modification research (Meichenbaum, 1977) and participative goal-setting research (Erez & Arad, 1986). Representative behaviors imply encouraging independent action, opportunity thinking, self-development, self-reward as well as using participative goal-setting and decision-making.

Macey and Schneider (2008) specified different definitions of Work Engagement. According to Schaufeli and Bakker (2004), Work Engagement is a positive, affective-motivational and work-related state that is characterized by vigor, dedication and absorption. Vigor refers to high levels of energy, the willingness to invest effort in one´s tasks and mental resilience while working. Dedication is characterized by a strong involvement in one´s work, accompanied by feelings of enthusiasm and significance and by a sense of inspiration and pride. Absorption refers to a pleasant state of total captivation in one´s work, which is characterized by time passing quickly and being unable to disengage oneself from the it. Work Engagement can be enhanced by autonomy and responsibility, social support and coaching, performance feedback, high levels of perceived fairness as well as task variety (these aspects can be developed by empowerment).

Empowering Leadership can play an intrinsic and an extrinsic motivational role to stimulate engagement. Intrinsically, Empowering Leadership behavior facilitates employees meet the fundamental need for self-determination and control (Ryan & Deci, 2000). By encouraging followers to use self-rewards, allow for follower self-leadership, engaging in participative goal-setting and encouraging teamwork as well as independent action, empowering leaders transfer power to their subordinates (Manz & Sims, 1987). In doing so, they foster followers' capacity for self-determination and feelings of mastery, which in turn, reduce change-related stressors, such as fear or mistrust. Extrinsically, the outcome of an increased feeling of mastery and self-determination fosters motivation for task accomplishment (Conger & Kanungo, 1988). Due to delegation, consultation and support, this enhanced level of motivation is combined with the capacity to succeed and achieve work- as well as change-related goals.

Thus, Empowering Leadership is supposed to foster Employee Work Engagement via intrinsic and extrinsic motivational processes, which leads to the first assumption.

Hypothesis 1: There is a direct positive relationship between Empowering Leadership and Employee Work Engagement.

2.2 The Mediating Roles of Self-Efficacy

According to Baron and Kenny (1986), the role of Self-Efficacy (SLF in the following) as a mediator of the EL - WE relationship is supported, in part, by the links between: (1) EL and WE, (2) EL and SLF, (3) SLF and WE. The mentioned links, except the link between EL and WE, which was discussed above, are discussed as follows.

2.2.1 Empowering Leadership and Self-Efficacy

As a key element in Bandura's (1977) theory of social learning, SLF refers to an individual's belief in his or her capability to achieve a course of action needed to adhere the demands of a specific work situation. Bandura (1977) stated that SLF should not be conceptualized and measured in terms of generalized feelings of mastery, but rather in reference to dealing with a specific situation or performing a specific behavior. In regard with the Change Management Study, SLF is related to organizational change. Change-related SLF can be defined as an employee's perceived ability to function well on the job, despite the demands of a changing work environment (Wanberg & Banas, 2000). Employees who doubt their ability to respond to the demands of any organizational change event are more likely to focus attention on their feelings of incompetence, which will be accompanied by a sense of psychological distress and a failure to cope with the situation (Bandura, 1977). In contrast, employees who have high levels of change-related SLF are less likely to be distressed by a feeling of inadequacy. They are rather expected to persist in their efforts to tackle the organizational change process.

Bandura (1982) defined four sources of SLF: mastery experience, vicarious experience, verbal persuasion and emotional arousal. The present study expects EL to have an influence on each of the four sources. For example, an empowering leader can provide opportunities for mastery and vicarious experiences to his or her followers via verbal persuasion, encouragement and social inclusion. Previous research supports the contention, that empowering leaders can motivate employees in that they are able to meet expected outcomes (Tierney & Farmer, 2002). In other words, an empowering leader is perceived by his or her subordinates as a substantial organizational resource upon which they can rely when performing daily tasks. Specifically, in the context of organizational change, the perceived availability of EL may enhance employees' confidence, that the job will get done (i.e. high SLF).

Very few studies have tested the extent to which particular event characteristics are directly related to situational evaluations of control and SLF in the context of organizational change. An exception was a study conducted by Shaw et al. (1993), which was carried out at AT & T. Shaw et al. (1993) examined the extent to which certain characteristics of the change event (i.e. social support and open communication) were positively related to control appraisals (operationalized as job-related autonomy). As expected, both types, support and communication (deployed by the leader) were positively related to job-related autonomy. In turn, as already mentioned above, job-related autonomy leads to a higher sense of SLF.

An intermediate objective of this term paper is to investigate the role of change-related SLF as a personal resource fostered by EL behavior in an organizational change environment.

2.2.2 Self-Efficacy and Work Engagement

Generally, organizational change is intended to alter key organizational variables, that affect the members of the organization as well as their work-related attitudes and behaviors (Jimmieson, Terry & Callan, 2004). Organizational change processes can create uncertainty, fear and doubt (Graetz & Smith, 2010; Jaskyte, 2003), which, in turn, results in a tendency for employees to resist, avoid and devalue organizational change.

Prussia, Anderson & Manz (1998) assumed, that, the greater a person's SLF, the more confident he or she is about being successful in a difficult task domain (i.e. organizational change). In other words, SLF can have a critical effect on an individual's perceived readiness to carry out control in the workplace. Furthermore, employees with high levels of SLF are more likely to strive to accomplish difficult tasks and less prone to give up, when obstacles appear during organizational change (Schyns, 2004). Those who confidence to wield control and want to strive to ensure a successful implementation of the change event, are willing to do more than is required of them, even if it comes up to personal sacrifice (Meyer & Herscovitch, 2001; Meyer et al., 2007).

Accordingly, it is reasonable to conclude, that employees with high SLF are more likely to show higher levels of WE during organizational change.

Based on all the inferences previously discussed, EL is not only supposed to influence WE directly, but also indirectly via SLF.

Hypothesis 2: Self-Efficacy mediates the relationship between Empowering Leadership and Employee Work Engagement.

2.3 The Mediating Roles of Self-Esteem

Organizational-based Self-Esteem (SLS in the following) is defined as "the degree to which organizational members believe that they can satisfy their needs by participating in roles within the context of an organization" (Pierce et al., 1989, p. 625).

As SLS can be seen as a considerable personal resource, this variable was investigated as a mediator of the EL - WE relationship, in part, by the links between: (1) EL and WE, (2) EL and SLS, (3) SLS and WE. The mentioned links, except the link between EL and WE, which was discussed initially, are discussed as follows.

2.3.1 Empowering Leadership and Self-Esteem

According to Michel, Stemaier & Salvador (2010), individuals in organizations strive for a positive self-concept. Self-concept is derived from membership and from the way in which the group to which one belongs is valued by others (i.e. supervisor, coworkers and the organization). The ability of the leaders to create a feeling of employee self-responsibility makes employees feel a sense of personal control over their work and their activities within their work environment. In the context of organizational change, the perceived availability of EL may consequently enhance employees' confidence (higher SLS). EL allows subordinates to feel confident in their ability to deal with challenges and overcome change events successfully. Thus, one can expect a direct, positive relationship between EL and SLS.

2.3.2 Self-Esteem and Work Engagement

If employees feel a sense of personal control over their work and their activities, their SLS is strengthened, which in turn may foster their WE. Several researchers have investigated the relationships between personal resources and WE.

Rothmann and Storm (2003) conducted a large cross-sectional study among 1.910 South African police officers. They found, that engaged police-officers use an active coping style: They are problem-focused, taking active steps to make efforts to eliminate or rearrange stressors.

In their study among highly skilled Dutch technicians, Xanthopoulou et al. (2007a) examined the role of three personal resources (SLF, organizational-based SLS and Optimism) in predicting WE. Results indicated, that engaged employees are highly self-efficacious (see also **2.2.2**); they believe that they can meet the demands they face in a wide range of contexts. In addition, engaged workers have the tendency to believe they can satisfy their needs by participating in roles within the organization (organizational-based SLS) (cf. Mauno et al., 2007). These findings were replicated and expanded in a two-year follow-up study (Xanthopoulou et al., 2007a). Findings showed, that organizational-based SLS as well as SLF contributed uniquely to explaining variance in WE over time, over and above the impact of job resources and previous levels of engagement.

As a final example, Bakker et al. (2007) in their study among female school principals found, that those with most personal resources (i.e. high SLS and high SLF) scored highest on WE.
Hence, a mediating effect of SLS between EL and WE was assumed to exist.

Hypothesis 3: Self-Esteem mediates the relationship between Empowering Leadership and Employee Work Engagement.

3 Method

3.1 Sample and Data Collection

The Change Management Study related to the question, to what extent personal resources are supposed to be important for the outcomes in the context of organizational change.

The cross-section analysis was conducted among employees from different lines of business in November and December 2016. Students from the University of Potsdam were asked to recruit employees who had just faced any kind of organizational change event in their work environment and who were willing to voluntarily participate in the survey. Every employee received an e-mail, in which the purpose of the study was briefly described, and in which they were requested to participate. The confidentiality and anonymity of their answers was emphasized and assured. For those who wished to participate, a link to the electronic questionnaire as well as an information sheet were included in the e-mail.

The questionnaire implied five generic categories: Questions about the Leader, Questions about the Follower him- or herself, Personality, Well-Being at the Workplace and General Questions. Questions about the Leader contained leadership behaviors, such as EL. Questions about the Follower implied Age, Gender, Education and the Big Five (short). SLF and SLS were classified as Personality variables. WE was part of the overall variable Well-Being at the Workplace. Among others, Sector and Job Tenure were considered as variables measuring General Questions. As this term paper put emphasis on EL, Well-Being and Personality, other variables are mostly disregarded in the following.

3.2 Measures

Multi-item scales were used to ensure adequate measurement of each variable. For the same reason, established scales were used where suitable. Reliability of the measures was assessed using Cronbach's α coefficient, these are presented in *Table 1* (see **Appendix**).

Organizational Change was assessed with an open-ended question. Participants were asked to briefly describe the change event they had been through.

Empowering Leadership was assessed through various dimensions, such as individual consideration, intellectual stimulation and motivation, using 8 items. Items include "Integrates me in important decision-making processes" and "Allows me to set own goals". The responses were measured along a 7-point Likert scale ranging from 1 ("strongly disagree") to 7 ("totally applicable") with respect to the respondent's certainty as to their immediate supervisor's leadership ability. The internal consistency of this scale was .868 in the current sample. As the Cronbach's α coefficient ranges from minus infinity to one, this is quite good.

Work Engagement was measured by 9-item scale. The scale items reflect three underlying dimensions, which are measured with three items each: *vigor* (e.g. "At my work, I feel bursting with energy"), *dedication* (e.g. "My job inspires me") and *absorption* (e.g. "I get carried away while working"). The responses were measured along a 5-point Likert scale ranging from 1 ("strongly disagree") to 5 ("strongly agree"). The internal consistency was .924 in the current sample, which is excellent.

Self-Efficacy was measured by 8-item scale. Items include "I am able to cope with challenges", "I will accomplish most of my goals" and "Even if circumstances are difficult, I can succeed". The responses were measured along a 5-point Likert scale ranging from 1 ("strongly disagree") to 5 ("strongly agree"). The internal consistency was .875 in the current sample, which is quite good.

Self-Esteem was measured by 10-item scale. Items include "All in all, I am satisfied with myself", "I have found a positive attitude towards myself" and "I consider myself as a valuable human". Responses were measured along a 5-point Likert scale ranging from 1 ("strongly disagree") to 5 ("strongly agree"). The internal consistency was .282 in the current sample, which is unacceptable. As the internal consistency measures whether several items, that propose to measure the same general construct, produce similar scores, the scale for SLS seemed to be inadequate in the current study.

In order to test the direct effect of EL on WE, a simple linear regression was conducted. The mediating effects were measured through multiple regression (see **4.2.2**). All data were analyzed with the SPSS statistical analysis program.

4 Results

4.1 Sample Characteristics

A total of 147 valid questionnaires were returned. Descriptive Statistics for the valid respondents are presented in *Table 2 and 3* below.

		Frequency (absolute)	Frequency (%)
Gender	Male	59	40,1
	Female	88	59,9
Age (years)	20-30	91	61,9
	31-40	25	17,0
	41-50	13	8,9
	> 50	18	12,2
Education	CSE	1	0,7
	GCSE	15	10,2
	High School	26	17,7
	University Degree	104	70,7
	Doctorate	1	0,7

Table 2: Descriptive Statistics – Frequencies (Gender, Age, Education)

	Means	Standard Deviation	Minimum	Maximum
Sex	1,60	,492	1	2
Age	32,64	10,745	20	65
Education	4,61	,708	2	6

Table 3: Descriptive Statistics (Gender, Age, Education)

88 participants were female and 59 participants were male, which made up a proportion of 59,9 % (female) to 40,1 % (male). Their age ranged from 20 to 65 years, which made up a span of 45. 62 % of the participants were between 20 and 30 years old, whereas only 12,2 % were older than 50. The average age was 32,64 years. Concerning the variable "Education", the University Degree was the most frequent (104 or 70,7 %). This was followed by the High School Diploma with a frequency of 26 (17,7 %), General Certificate of Secondary Education with a frequency of 15 and the Secondary School Leaving Certificate (CSE) as well as the Doctorate (1 or 0,7 % each).

4.2 Hypothesis Testing

Means, Standard Deviations, Intercorrelations and Internal Reliabilities among the variables are reported in *Table 4* (see below). Because of its unacceptable Cronbach´s α, SLS is put in brackets; possible causes and solution approaches are discussed subsequently. All other measures show high internal reliabilities, with coefficient α ranging from .868 to .924. The pattern of correlations is consistent with the hypothesized relationships (*Hypothesis 1* and *2*).

	M	SD	1	2	3	4
1 Empowering LS	5.051	1.075	(0.868)			
2 Work Engagement	4.335	0975	0.450**	(0.924)		
3 Self-Efficacy	4.017	0.487	0.299**	0.239**	(0.875)	
[4 Self-Esteem	2.980	0.312	- 0.003	0.076	0.055	(0.282)]

** p < 0.01.

Table 4: Means, Standard Deviations, Internal Consistencies (Cronbach's α on the diagonal) and Correlations among the variables (n = 147)

4.2.1 Direct Effect of Empowering Leadership on Work Engagement

In order to test the direct effect of EL on WE, a simple linear regression was conducted. The predictor variable EL was statistically significant, positive related to the outcome variable WE (0.450, $p < 0.01$). The coefficient of determination was 0.202, which means, that 20 % of the variance in WE could be explained by differences in the variance of EL. As the coefficient of determination ranges from zero to one, this was a solid prediction, but not of very high quality (cf. *Table 5, 6, 7* and *Figure 4* in the **Appendix**).

4.2.2 Mediating Effects of Self-Efficacy and Self-Esteem

The tests concerning the mediation effects formulated in *Hypothesis 2* and *3*, were derived from the approach of Baron and Kenny (1986). According to this method, there are four steps in establishing a significant mediation effect. First, there must be a significant relationship between the predictor and the outcome (cf. **4.2.1**). Second, the predictor (EL) must be significantly related to the mediator (SLF, SLS). Third, the mediator (SLF, SLS) should be significantly related to the outcome variable (WE). Finally, a significant mediation effect exists, when the relationship between the predictor and the outcome has become significantly weaker (partial mediation) or non-significant (full mediation), after the inclusion of the mediator.

The first condition was proved (cf. **4.2.1**). Further, EL had a statistically significant, positive relationship with the potential mediator SLF (0.299, $p < 0.01$). Moreover, SLF had a statistically significant, positive relationship with WE (0.239, $p < 0.01$). As the mediating variable (SLF) accounts for some, but not all of the relationship between the independent variable (EL) and the dependent variable (WE), a partial mediation was assumed to exist. Thus, there is not only a significant relationship between SLF and WE, but also some direct relationship between EL and WE (cf. **4.2.1** and *Table 10* in the **Appendix**).

EL had no statistically significant effect on SLS (-0.003, $p < 0.01$) in the present study. Besides, SLS had no statistically significant effect on WE (0.076, $p < 0.01$). Consequently, *Hypothesis 3* had to be rejected in the current study (cf. *Table 13* in the **Appendix**).

5 Discussion

The assumed model presented in this study demonstrated, that in the context of organizational change, EL is important in a way of fostering employees' WE directly and indirectly, by enhancing employees' SLF. Additionally, the findings indicated that EL functions as a means of enhancing control felt over some aspects of job demands (i.e. organizational change), which, in turn, could foster WE. That emphasizes the importance of EL in developing employees' personal resources (i.e. SLF) and behaviors (i.e. WE), in order to facilitate organizational change. In short, EL fosters individuals' SLF to exert behavioral efforts (high WE), which, as a result, contributes to their organization's successful implementation of change.

EL and WE contributed significantly in explaining the elemental psychological mechanisms of the motivational process of the JD-R model. Traditionally, job resources (leadership behavior in this case) are seen as instrumental for employees to fulfill their work tasks, which consequently keep employees engaged in their job (Hakanen et al., 2006; Schaufeli & Bakker, 2004). This study went one step further by showing that the work environment as well as the supply of job resources, both, activate employees' personal resources (SLF) and make them feel more capable to control and overcome the organizational change event (Luthans et al., 2006).

The investigated links are summarized in a Final Model (see *Figure 5*).

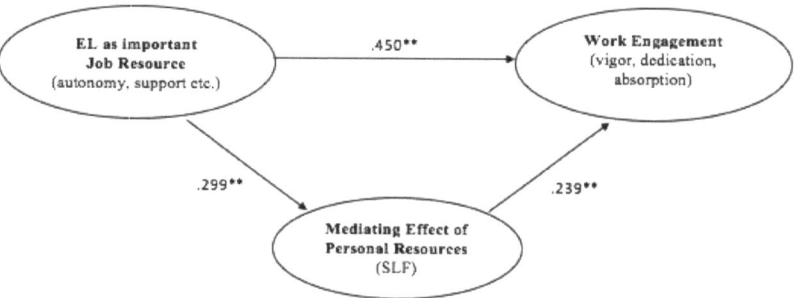

Figure 5: Final Model (Partial Mediation)

The rejection of *Hypothesis 3* concerning the mediating effect of SLS might be attributed to the nature of the specific Personality items included in the current study. As the internal consistency of the SLS scale was unacceptable, the selected scale and its items might not have been appropriated. It might be, that SLS operates mainly at an affective-cognitive level and less at a behavioral-practical level. Possibly, people differ between SLS as a personality trait and SLS in an organizational-based context. In this case, respondents might have mistaken the difference between those two constructs. Moreover, Gardner & Peirce (1998) stated, that although SLS and SLF are distinct, they are both related theoretically. Thus, there might be some latent intercorrelations between SLF and SLS, which, in turn, could have distorted the effects of SLS in the current study.

6 Limitations and Future Research Directions

According to the weaknesses mentioned above, the Change Management Study had some limitations that need to be acknowledged.

First, as already mentioned, the SLS scale had relatively low reliability estimates and thus constrained the findings. SLS might have a direct significant impact on the outcome variable WE, which could have been proven in other studies (cf. **2.3**). However, that correlation was discounted in this case as the measures were less reliable and not statistically significant. The same applies to the relationship between EL and SLS. To finally reject or yet confirm those effects, new studies should be deployed. Regarding the direction for future research, the roles of the numerous personal resources should be investigated and put in comparison to better recognize relevant mediating effects.

Second, while the multiple regression used for the analyses informs about possible direction of effects, the cross-sectional nature of the study limited conclusions about the causal relationships among the variables. Moreover, even though it could have been shown, that job resources (provided by EL) and personal resources (SLF) may be reciprocal, the research design precluded conclusions regarding the sequence of the stated effects. At the same time, little is known about the differential effects of various aspects of organizational factors on different elements of the attitudes of those individuals affected by change (Fedor et al., 2006).

Longitudinal designs are necessary to validate the findings over time and to provide insights regarding causality.

Furthermore, the current study was only based on self-report measures, which might lead to common method variance problems (self-report bias). However, it can be argued that constructs as *Personality* and *Work Engagement* are nearly impossible to measure in any other way than by self-reports (Mäkikangas et al., 2004).

Finally, the sample was confined to a limited number of 147 participants, which in turn limits the generalizability of its findings and conclusions. Regarding future research directions, larger sample sizes are necessary to secure representativeness.

7 Conclusion

This term paper highlighted the relationship between EL and Employee WE in organizational change processes. Despite its limitations, the Change Management Study came up with several strengths.

First, there had been a lack of empirical research on the role of EL in a change context per se. In this regard, the present study filled the gap by conducting an empirical research. The results indicate, that EL has significant and powerful influence on employees' supportive attitudes and behavior vis-à-vis organizational change (high levels of WE).

Moreover, the study provided additional insight into the mechanisms through which EL influences Employee WE for organizational change. SLF was found to be an important mediator concerning the EL - WE relationship, which in turn means that supervisors who are confronted with the task of leading through a specific change event can foster their followers´ WE by developing Employee SLF.

To sum up, personal resources (e.g. SLF) are considered to be of high value in the context of managing (i.e. EL) and performing (i.e. WE) organizational change (Graetz & Smith, 2010; Kool & van Dierendonck, 2012). But still, there is considerable room for investigating the contributions of the various personal resources regarding the EL - WE relationship.

Appendix

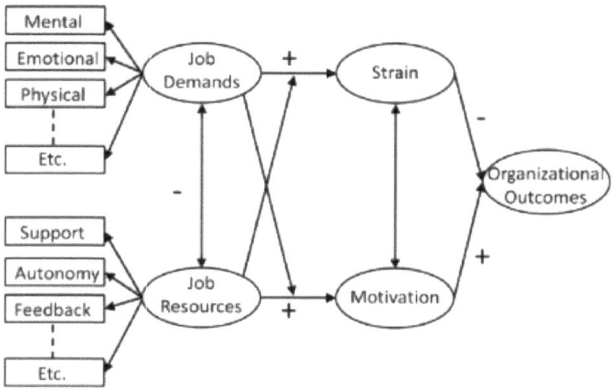

Figure 1: The JD-R Model (van den Heuvel et al., 2009, p. 126)

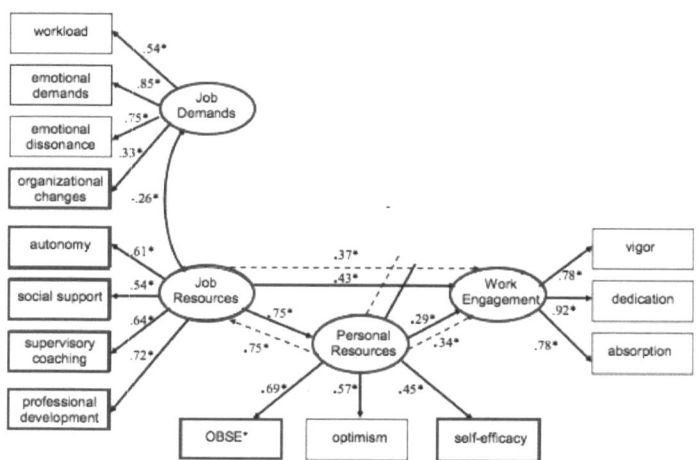

* p = .001

Figure 2: The expanded JD-R Model (in part) by Xanthopoulou et al. (2007, p. 135)

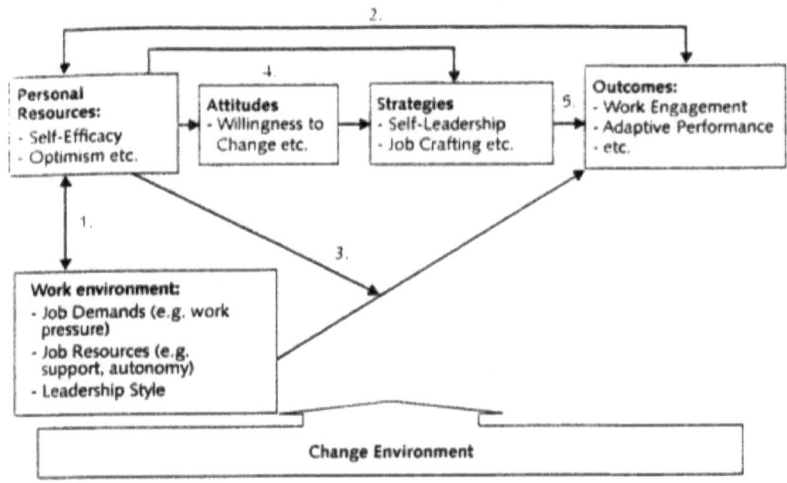

Figure 3: The Personal Resources Adaption Model by van den Heuvel et al. (2009, p. 138)

	Cronbach´s α	Number of Items
Empowering Leadership	.868	8
Self-Esteem	.282	10
Self-Efficacy	.875	8
Work Engagement	.924	9

Table 1: Internal Consistency: Cronbach´s alpha

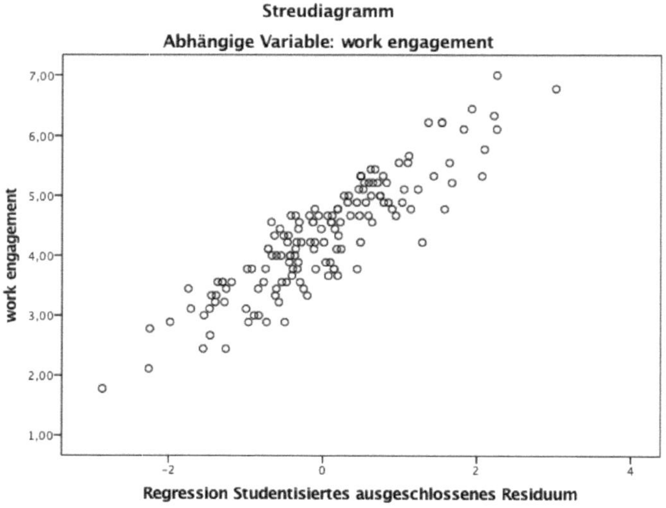

Figure 4: Scatterplot of the EL – WE Relationship (SPSS-Output)

Modellzusammenfassung[b]

Modell	R	R-Quadrat	Korrigiertes R-Quadrat	Standardfehler des Schätzers
1	,450[a]	,202	,197	,85785

a. Einflußvariablen : (Konstante), empowering leadership
b. Abhängige Variable: work engagement

p = .05

Table 5: Linear Regression - Direct Effect of EL on WE (Overall Model)

ANOVA[a]

Modell		Quadratsumme	df	Mittel der Quadrate	F	Sig.
1	Regression	27,071	1	27,071	36,786	,000[b]
	Nicht standardisierte Residuen	106,706	145	,736		
	Gesamt	133,777	146			

a. Abhängige Variable: work engagement
b. Einflußvariablen : (Konstante), empowering leadership

p = .05

Table 6: Linear Regression - Direct Effect of EL on WE (ANOVA)

Koeffizienten[a]

Modell		Nicht standardisierte Koeffizienten		Standardisierte Koeffizienten	T	Sig.
		RegressionskoeffizientB	Standardfehler	Beta		
1	(Konstante)	2,294	,344		6,672	,000
	empowering leadership	,404	,067	,450	6,065	,000

a. Abhängige Variable: work engagement

p = .05

Table 7: Linear Regression - Direct Effect of EL on WE (Coefficients)

Modellzusammenfassung[b]

Modell	R	R-Quadrat	Korrigiertes R-Quadrat	Standardfehler des Schätzers
1	,463[a]	,214	,203	,85431

a. Einflußvariablen : (Konstante), self-efficacy, empowering leadership

b. Abhängige Variable: work engagement

p = .05

Table 8: Linear Regression - Effect of SLF on EL and WE (Overall Model)

ANOVA[a]

Modell		Quadratsumme	df	Mittel der Quadrate	F	Sig.
1	Regression	28,679	2	14,340	19,647	,000[b]
	Nicht standardisierte Residuen	105,098	144	,730		
	Gesamt	133,777	146			

a. Abhängige Variable: work engagement

b. Einflußvariablen : (Konstante), self-efficacy, empowering leadership

p = .05

Table 9: Linear Regression - Effect of SLF on EL and WE (ANOVA)

Koeffizienten[a]

Modell		Nicht standardisierte Koeffizienten		Standardisierte Koeffizienten	T	Sig.	95,0% Konfidenzintervalle für B	
		RegressionskoeffizientB	Standardfehler	Beta			Untergrenze	Obergrenze
1	(Konstante)	1,543	,611		2,527	,013	,336	2,751
	empowering leadership	,373	,070	,416	5,369	,000	,236	,511
	self-efficacy	,226	,152	,115	1,484	,140	-,075	,526

a. Abhängige Variable: work engagement

p = .05

Table 10: Linear Regression - Effect of SLF on EL and WE (Coefficients)

Modellzusammenfassung[b]

Modell	R	R-Quadrat	Korrigiertes R-Quadrat	Standardfehler des Schätzers
1	,456[a]	,208	,197	,85757

a. Einflußvariablen : (Konstante), self-esteem, empowering leadership

b. Abhängige Variable: work engagement

$p = .05$

Table 11: Linear Regression - Effect of SLS on EL and WE (Overall Model)

ANOVA[a]

Modell		Quadratsumme	df	Mittel der Quadrate	F	Sig.
1	Regression	27,877	2	13,938	18,953	,000[b]
	Nicht standardisierte Residuen	105,901	144	,735		
	Gesamt	133,777	146			

a. Abhängige Variable: work engagement

b. Einflußvariablen : (Konstante), self-esteem, empowering leadership

$p = .05$

Table 12: Linear Regression - Effect of SLS on EL and WE (ANOVA)

Koeffizienten[a]

Modell		Nicht standardisierte Koeffizienten		Standardisierte Koeffizienten	T	Sig.	95,0% Konfidenzintervalle für B	
		RegressionskoeffizientB	Standardfehler	Beta			Untergrenze	Obergrenze
1	(Konstante)	1,585	,760		2,085	,039	,082	3,087
	empowering leadership	,404	,067	,450	6,070	,000	,273	,536
	self-esteem	,238	,227	,078	1,047	,297	-,211	,687

a. Abhängige Variable: work engagement

$p = .05$

Table 13: Linear Regression - Effect of SLS on EL and WE (Coefficients)

List of Literature

Arnold, J., Aarad, S., Rhoades, J. A. & Drasgow, F. (2000). The empowering leadership questionnaire: The construction and validation of a new scale for measuring leader behaviors. *Journal of Organizational Behavior*, 21 (3), 249-269.

Bandura, A. (1977). Self-efficacy: Toward a unifying theory of behavioral change. *Psychological Review, 84* (2), 191-215.

Bandura, A. (1982). Self-efficacy mechanism in human agency. *American Psychologist*, 37, 122-147.

Bandura, A. (1986). The social foundations of thought and action: A social cognitive theory. Englewood Cliffs, NJ: Prentice Hall.

Bakker, A. B. & Demerouti, E. (2007). The Job Demands-Resources Model: state of the art. *Journal of Managerial Psychology*, 22 (3), 309-328.

Bakker, A. B., Hakanen, J. J. & Demerouti, E. & Xanthopoulou, D. (2007). Job Resources Boost Work Engagement. *Journal of Educational Psychology*, 99 (2), 234-284.

Baron, R. M. & Kenny, D. A. (1986). The moderator-mediator variable distinction in social psychological research: Conceptual, strategic and statistical considerations. *Journal of Personality and Social Psychology*, 51, 1173-1182.

Conger, J. A. and Kanungo, R.N. (1988). The Empowerment Process: Integrating Theory and Practice. *Academy of Management Review*, 13, 471-482.

Erez, M. & Arad, R. (1986). Participative goal setting; Social, motivational, and cognitive factors. *Journal of Applied Psychology,* 71, 591-597.

Fedor, D. B., Caldwell, S. & Herold, D. M. (2006). The effects of organizational changes on employee commitment: A multilevel investigation. *Personnel Psychology,* 59 (1), 1-29.

Gardner, D. G. & Peirce, J. L. (1998). Self-Esteem and Self-Efficacy within the Organizational Context. *Group & Organization Management,* 23 (1), 48-70.

Graetz, F. & Smith, A. C. T. (2010). Managing Organizational Change: A Philosophies of Change Approach. *Journal of Change Management,* 10 (2), 135-154.

Hakanen, J., Bakker, A. B. & Schaufeli, W. B. (2006). Burnout and work engagement among teachers. *Journal of School Psychology*, 43, 495–513.

Higgs, M. & Rowland, D. (2005). All Changes Great and Small: Exploring Approaches to Change and its Leadership. *Journal of Change Management*, 5 (2), 121-151, June 2005.

Hobfoll, S. E., Johnson, R. J., Ennis, N. & Jackson, A. P. (2003). Resource loss, resource gain, and emotional outcomes among inner city women. *Journal of Personality and Social Psychology,* 84, 632–643.

Jaskyte, K. (2003). Assessing Changes in Employees' perceptions of Leadership Behavior, job Design, and organizational Arrangements and their job satisfaction and commitment. *Administration in Social Work,* 27 (4), 25-39.

Jaros, S. (2010). Commitment to Organizational Change: A Critical Review. *Journal of Change Management*, 10 (1), 79-108.

Jimmieson, N. L., Terry, D. J. & Callan, V. J. (2004). A Longitudinal Study of Employee Adaptation to Organizational Change: The Role of Change-Related Information and Change-Related Self-Efficacy. *Journal of Occupational Health Psychology*, 9 (1), 11-27.

Kirkman, B. L. & Rosen, B. 1999. Beyond self-manage- ment: The antecedents and consequences of team empowerment. *Academy of Management Journal,* (42), 58-74.

Kool, M. & van Dierendonck, D. (2012). Servant leadership and commitment to change, the mediating role of justice and optimism. *Journal of Organizational Change Management*, 25, 422–433.

Lamm, E. & Gordon, J. R. (2010). Empowerment, Predisposition to Resist Change, and Support for Organizational Change. *Journal of Leadership & Organizational Studies*, 17 (4), 426-437.

Luthans, F., Avey, J. B., Avolio, B. J., Norman, S. M. & Combs, G. M. (2006). Psychological capital development: Toward a micro-intervention. *Journal of Organizational Behavior, 27,* 387–393.

Macey, W. H., & Schneider, B. (2008). The meaning of employee engagement. Industrial and Organizational Psychology. *Perspectives on Science and Practice*, 1, 3-30.

Mahoney, M. J., & Thoresen, C. E. (1974). *Self-control: Power to the person*. Monterey. CA: Brooks/Cole.

Mäkikangas, A., Kinnunen, U. & Feldt, T. (2004). Self-esteem, dispositional optimism, and health: Evidence from cross-lagged data on employees. *Journal of Research in Personality,* 38, 556 - 575.

Manz, C. C. & Sims, H. P. (1987). Leading workers to lead themselves. The external leadership of self-managing work teams. *Administrative Science Quarterly*, 32, 106-129.

Mauno, S., Kinnunen, U. & Ruokolainen, M. (2007). Job demands and resources as antecedents of work engagement: a longitudinal study. *Journal of Organizational Behavior*, 70, 149-71.

Meichenbaum, D. H. (1977). *Cognitive behavior modification: An integrative approach.* New York: Plenum.

Meyer, J. P. & Herscovitch, L. (2001). Commitment in the workplace Toward a general model. *Human Resource Management Review,* 11 (3), 299-326.

Meyer, J. P., Srinivas, E. S., Lai, J. B. & Topolnytsky, L. (2007). Employee commitment and support for an organizational change: test of the three-component model in tow culture. *Journal of Occupational and Organizational Psychology,* 80 (2), 185-211.

Michel, A., Stemaier, R. & Salvador, R. (2010). I Scratch Your Back - You Scratch Mine. Do Procudural Justice and Orgnaizational Idenfication Matter for Employees' Cooperation During Change? *Journal of change management,* 10 (1), 41-59.

Parish, J. T., Cadwallader, S. & Busch, P. (2007). Want, need to ought to: employee commitment to organizational change. *Journal of Organizational Change Management,* 21(1), 32-52.

Pierce, J. L. & Gardner, D. G. (2004). Self-esteem within the work and organizational context: A review of the organizational-based self-esteem literature. *Journal of Management, 30,* 591– 622.

Pierce, J. L., Gardner, D. G., Cummings, L. L. & Dunham, R. B. (1989). Organizational-based self-esteem: Construct definition, measurement, and validation. *Academy of Management Journal,* 32, 622–648.

Prussia, G. E., Anderson, J. S. & Manz, C. C. (1998). Self-leadership and performance outcomes: The mediating influence of self-efficacy. *Journal of Organizational Behavior*, 19, 523-538.

Rothmann, S. & Storm, K. (2003). Work engagement in the South African Police Service. Paper presented at the *11th European Congress of Work and Organizational Psychology*, Lisbon.

Ryan, R. M. & Deci, E. L. (2000). Intrinsic and Extrinsic Motivations: Classic Definitions and New Directions. *Contemporary Educational Psychology*, (25), 54-67.

Shaw, J. B., Fields, M. W., Thacker, J. W. & Fisher, C. D. (1993). The availability of personal and external coping resources: Their impact on job stress and employee attitudes during organizational restructuring. *Work & Stress.,* 7, 229-246.

Schyns, B. (2004). The Influence of Occupational self-efficacy on the Relationship of Leadership Behavior and Preparedness for Occupational Change. *Journal of Career Development*, 30 (4), 247-261.

Tierney, P. & Farmer, S. M. (2002). Creative self-efficacy: Its potential antecedents and relationship to creative performance. *Academy of Management Journal*, 45, 1137–1148.

Van den Heuvel, M., Demerouti, E., Schreurs, B. H. J., Bakker, A. B. & Schaufeli, W. B. (2009). Does meaning-making help during organizational change? Development and validation of a new scale. *Career Development International,* 14 (6), 508-533.

Wanberg, C. R. & Banas, J. T. (2000). Predictors and Outcomes of Openness to Changes in a Reorganizing Workplace. *Journal of Applied Psychology*, 85, 132-142.

Xanthopoulou, D., Bakker, A. B., Demerouti, E. & Schaufeli, W. B. (2007). The Role of Personal Resources in the Job Demands-Resources Model. *International Journal of Stress Management*, 14 (2), 121–141.

Xanthopoulou, D., Bakker, A. B., Demerouti, E. & Schaufeli, W. B. (2007a). The role of personal resources in the job demands-resources model. *International Journal of Stress Management,* 14, 121-41.

Yousef, D. A. (2000). Organizational commitment and job satisfaction as predictors of attitudes toward organizational change in a non-western setting. *Personnel review,* 29 (5), 567-592.